I KNOW THE SEASONS

By Jon Welzen

Gareth Stevens
PUBLISHING

first concepts

I know
the four seasons.

The four seasons
are winter, spring,
summer, and fall.

winter

spring

summer

fall

5

Winter is cold.

I see snow in winter.

9

Spring is rainy.

I see new plants
in spring.

Summer is hot.

15

I swim in summer.

17

Fall is cool.

19

I see many colors
of leaves in fall.

21

What season
do you like best?

23

Please visit our website, www.garethstevens.com. For a free color catalog of all our high-quality books, call toll free 1-800-542-2595 or fax 1-877-542-2596.

Cataloging-in-Publication Data

Names: Welzen, Jon.
Title: I know the seasons / Jon Welzen.
Description: New York : Gareth Stevens Publishing, 2017. | Series: What I know
Identifiers: ISBN 9781482454734 (pbk.) | ISBN 9781482454758 (library bound) | ISBN 9781482454741 (6 pack)
Subjects: LCSH: Seasons–Juvenile literature.
Classification: LCC QB637.4 W45 2017 | DDC 508.2–dc23

First Edition

Published in 2017 by
Gareth Stevens Publishing
111 East 14th Street, Suite 349
New York, NY 10003

Designer: Sarah Liddell
Editor: Therese Shea

Photo credits: Cover, p. 1 (stripes) Eky Studio/Shutterstock.com; cover, p. 1 (seasons) Piotr Krzeslak/Shutterstock.com; p. 3 pavelgr/Shutterstock.com; p. 5 Ingrid Prats/Shutterstock.com; p. 7 Pressmaster/Shutterstock.com; p. 9 Kotenko Oleksandr/Shutterstock.com; p. 11 wanphen chawarung/Shutterstock.com; p. 13 Sofiawood/Shutterstock.com; p. 15 loskutnikov/Shutterstock.com; p. 17 Tom Wang/Shutterstock.com; p. 19 Jacek Chabraszewski/Shutterstock.com; p. 21 Anna Moskvina/Shutterstock.com; p. 23 GoodMood Photo/Shutterstock.com.

Printed in the United States of America

CPSIA compliance information: Batch #CW17GS: For further information contact Gareth Stevens, New York, New York at 1-800-542-2595.